500 Halloween Costume Ideas

Costume and Cosplay ideas for Boys, Girls, Men, Women, Cats, and Dogs

Jen Stokes

Copyright © 2018 by Jen Stokes

All rights reserved. No part of this publication may be reproduced, distributed, or transmitted in any form or by any means, including photocopying, recording, or other electronic or mechanical methods, without the prior written permission of the publisher, except in the case of brief quotations embodied in critical reviews and certain other noncommercial uses permitted by copyright law.

Introduction

Hello, and welcome to my fun list of ideas for Halloween or any other event where the host is all excited it's a costume party but you're silently fuming/panicking because you don't have anything to wear.

Dressing up is fun. If you're not having fun, you're wearing the wrong costume.

Some of the ideas on this list might be difficult to replicate. Those are there to get your creative juices flowing. Try using a random number generator and combining a few entries.

Be creative and have fun. Those are the only rules for costumes. – *Jen Stokes*

1. Sharknado

2. Plastic green army men

3. Bigfoot

4. Batman vs. Superman

5. Waldo from *Where's Waldo?*

6. Fried egg

7. Lady Gaga's meat dress

8. A giant cupcake

9. A sack of potatoes

10. Rainbow zebra

11. Taco Bell dog

12. Beauty and the Beast

13. Mad Max

14. Captain Hook

15. The alligator that ate Captain Hook

16. Evil Link from the Zelda series

17. A bar of soap

18. Rowboat with holes in it

19. Trapped in an oil painting

20. The ghost of Christmas Futurama

21. Alien cowboy

22. The xenomorph from that movie *Alien*

23. Snow globe

24. Person being carried

25. Extra head

26. Person dragging around a zombie

27. The very hungry caterpillar

28. Nemo and Dory

29. Alice in Wonderbread Land

30. Rock and Rolling Pin

31. Steampunk wizard

32. Fire truck

33. The logo of your favorite company

34. Bus driver who's always late

35. Ronald McDonald

36. Mario and Luigi

37. Princess Nectarine the long-lost cousin of Princess Peach

38. Gordon Ramsay and beleaguered kitchen staff

39. A mouse trap

40. Bowling pin

41. Gingerbread cookie

42. Lazy dwarf

43. The dragons from *Game of Thrones*

44. Stone gargoyle

45. Michelangelo, famous painter and ninja turtle.

46. Jack Skellington

47. The heroine from *Kill Bill* with the samurai sword

48. Helicopter exploding in a movie

49. Lobster knife fight

50. Ghostbusters

51. Anybody from *Tron* with cool glow stuff on them

52. A half-empty glass of milk

53. Hawaiian Santa Claus

54. Rudolph the reindeer that drank too much

55. An Amazon package

56. Flaming Carrot

57. Solvable Rubik's cube

58. Forklift

59. Garbage can you can fold yourself into and scare people

60. Umbrella monster

61. A list of Halloween costume ideas

62. 50 Shades of any color except for grey.

63. Crayon person

64. An Etch-A-Sketch

65. Bitcoin ATM

66. Samurai Darth Vader

67. Steve from Minecraft

68. LEGO head person

69. Modern day pirate

70. Lawyer that charges a lot but doesn't win cases

71. British judge

72. Overwatch character in beach attire

73. Baseball player past his prime

74. BLT sandwich

75. Headless Horseman

76. An Oscar statue

77. Wikipedia entry

78. Go Fund Me page for next year's Halloween costume

79. Functional pawn shop

80. Care Bear motorcycle gang

81. Bebop and Rocksteady

82. A flock of birds

83. Dung beetle

84. Master Chief from *Halo* but give him a unique color

85. 60s square-head robot

86. Horse with carrot dangling from a stick

87. Pacman and ghost buddies

88. Flushable port-a-potty

89. The DVD box set of *Harry Potter*

90. Zombie cat or other cute animal

91. Genie on a flying carpet

92. Redneck version of your favorite Disney character

93. IRS tax agent here to audit you

94. Thunder and lightning

95. Space cowboy

96. Pet detective

97. Starship Trooper

98. Duke Nukem

99. Dinosaur covered in feathers which is probably what they really looked like

100. Yukon gold miner

101. Ugly lamp

102. Murdered and rolled up in a carpet

103. Dog playing poker

104. Can of tuna fish

105. Bottle of suntan lotion

106. Box of Kleenex

107. Pool shark

108. Poker table

109. King Kong on the Empire State Building swatting at fighter jets

110. A jammed printer

111. Swamp monster

112. Escaped convict who shows up with flowers

113. Your favorite emoticon

114. Mega Man and Zero

115. One of Bowser's annoying kids.

116. Expensive dining room table set

117. Plastic cutlery man

118. Dude where's my car?

119. Woodpecker

120. Cat o' nine tails

121. Claw machine with prizes you can win

122. Jigsaw puzzle with a single missing piece

123. Egyptian mummy

124. Komodo dragon

125. VCR machine

126. Those freaky twins from *The Shining*

127. That freaky guy who wrote *The Shining*

128. Justin Beaver-Bieber

129. A popular hastag

130. Cold turkey

131. An older meme that still checks out

132. Box of macaroni and cheese

133. Pumpkin head

134. Rotten fish

135. Leak in brand new roof

136. A ton of student debt

137. The Queen of England but if she were an anime character

138. Angry Birds merchandise that ended up in a dumpster

139. Bouquet of candy flowers

140. Allergy season

141. Pirate and parrot

142. Goldilocks and the Chicago Bears

143. Those grumpy old guys from the *Muppets*

144. Kermit after he snaps

145. Zombie Easter bunny

146. Rave attire vampire

147. Dothraki wedding disaster

148. A cheap hotel room

149. Stuck in an elevator

150. Flood water

151. Ninja the Fortnite streamer

152. Gunslinger

153. Political corruption

155. The entire Simpsons family even the dog

156. Cowardly Lion but super buff

157. Wonder Woman if she went bad

158. Robin takes over Wayne Manor in a violent coup

159. Marvel vs Capcom

160. Chess piece

161. Several donkeys

162. Animal head on a wall

163. Johnny Cash after rehab

165. WW2 zombie soldier

166. Megalodon

167. The planet Tatooine from *Star Wars*

168. Large French fries

169. Hurricane [YOUR NAME]

170. Post-apocalyptic Paris

171. Pod-racing mechanic

172. The Red Barron but he faked his death

173. A Jedi that can't decide which side he's on

174. Tugboat captain

175. Sailor with giant forearms that's not Popeye

176. Empty yogurt container

177. Classroom chalkboard

178. You get a bunch of those costumes for cats and make a patchwork one for yourself

179. Battle droid

180. Ghost of yourself

181. Slot machine that pays out

182. Too much hair

183. Big time solar eclipse

182. Chunks of Elvis' house

183. Angel wings

184. Too legit to quit

185. New Orleans is sinking and you don't want to swim in flood water because it's dangerous

186. Maid who steals things

187. Butler who catches her but lets her off the hook

188. Mutant bumblebee with two stingers

189. The cast of Chrono Trigger

190. Steam-powered toaster

191. Turkey dog

192. Deep cover Russian spy

193. Snowing in July

194. Rat

195. Galaxy cake

196. 90s hip-hop star that nobody remembers

197. Boring painting that sold for millions

198. DC Comics movie

199. Five-star Yelp review

200. American Space Force

201. Fire golem scarecrow

202. Ice cream cone

203. Joker from Batman except this time he's a good guy

204. Paladin that went bad

205. Gorilla glue

206. Used car salesman

207. Beach drinks

208. Civil war canon

209. Hard to spell word

210. Bride of Ballpark Franks'entstein

211. The final shootout in a sweet action movie

212. Spooky clown car

213. Set of weights

214. Romantic comedy movie

215. Second chance

216. Useless golf pro

217. Dapper bank robber

218. Stunt car driver

219. Ugly casino pit boss

220. Retires super hero

221. Pulitzer prize for awesome

222. Not everything makes sense, Karen

223. Exercise equipment

224. Fictional sports team member

225. Harry Pottery Barn

226. Quidditch stuff

227. Expensive makeup

228. High paid female athlete

229. Social media manager

230. Dad jokes

231. Reality TV star that becomes leader of country

232. Eccentric CEO of electric car company

233. Stock certificate

234. Country western Barbie

235. Acoustic guitar

236. Budweiser beer commercial with horses

237. Manic newscaster

238. Noir movie characters

239. Early morning fishing

240. Deer that hunts people

241. Devil vs. fiddle player

242. Stock market crash

243. Forrest Gump and Bubba

244. Mechanized Richard Nixon

245. Restaurant meal with incorrect calorie count listed

246. Head in a jar

247. Honey bee apocalypse

248. Cyborg grandmother

249. Whale gets its revenge on a sharkfin boat

250. Fishing with dynamite

251. Public speaking expert

252. Roman gladiator

253. Hotdog salesman

254. Person who hands out candy to strangers

255. Hot wings and sour cream

256. The Incredibles family

257. Comic book villain that gets caught monologuing

258. Gru and minions

259. Mr. Freeze-y, the popsicle/Batman villain

260. A humongous frog

261. Cockroach

262. Chicken that doesn't want to become McNuggets

263. Decapitated French noble

264. Mickey Mouse, axe-murdering psychopath

265. Bag of popcorn

266. Person at the movies who won't stop using their phone

267. Figure skating legend, Tonya Harding

268. Professor Plumb-er

269. Lots of socks

270. Glue-eating toddler

271. Person who enjoys cleaning bathrooms

272. Preschool witch teacher

273. Igor, the hunchbacked assistant of Dr. Frankenstein

274. Canada

275. Moose centaur

276. Hippie in a tree

277. Bull whip archaeologist

278. Flickering light in a scary movie

279. Scream mask but painted

280. Character from a game cosplaying as a normal human

281. Yoda and his made-up wife

282. Time-travelling big game hunter

283. Tiger attack victim

284. The 500th Jurassic Park sequel

285. Too much peanut butter

286. Mermaid and Merman

287. Blue lobster

288. Aquafina Man

289. Annoying spokesperson for company nobody likes

290. Save money by switching car insurance

291. Furniture that won't fit through a door

292. Gangster with briefcase locked to wrist

293. Surfer turtle

294. Dentist who hurts people

295. Apple farmer

296. Garage band rock star

297. Cooking show host

298. Person covered in fake tattoos

299. ZZ top or Duck Dynasty beards

300. Shot through the heart

301. The Scooby Doo Gang

302. Top Gun pilot

303. Functional tank

304. Bazooka Joe

305. Shrek and Fiona

306. Roller coaster

307. College freshman

308. R2D2 and C-3PO

309. 80s horror movie marathon

310. Paint night

311. Wayne and Garth from *Wayne's World*

312. Dumb and Dumber

313. Reverse Snow White and Evil Queen

314. Eaten by a shark

315. Living in mom's basement

316. A phone book

317. Octopus

318. Jawas from *Star Wars*

319. Viking warrior with goofy foam axe

320. London Symphony Orchestra

321. Alf

322. The Lone Ranger

323. Fire and ice elemental combination surprise

324. Famous assassination attempt

325. Fake moon landing

326. Tabaco Chewbacca

327. Princess Leia with pastry rolls for hair buns

328. High school chemistry

329. Cola wars

330. Crumbling nationwide infrastructure

331. Caveman with dinosaur drumstick

332. The Garden of Eden but extremely evil

333. Fairy Godfather

334. Expensive dinnerware

335. Clumsy surgeon

336. Half man, half bear, half pig.

337. Robotic Godzilla

338. A giant spider with a tiny person riding him

339. The Monkey King

340. Terracotta warriors

341. The car from *Back to the Future*

342. Jack Frost experiments with fire

343. Pineapple chunks

344. Fire hydrant

345. Stop, hammer time

346. Buddhist monk

347. Coral reef

348. Deep sea exploration submarine

349. Way too much carpet

350. The worst character from *Parks and Recreation*

351. Spaghetti and meatballs

352. YouTube playlist

353. Snapchat

354. Functional iPad

355. Albert Einstein

356. Ripley and yellow power loader from *Aliens*

357. Groot and you have to stay in character all night.

358. Young Gandalf

359. Old Harry Potter

360. Poison birthday cake

361. A three person political debate with unique platforms

362. Patient who had the wrong limb amputated

363. Fingernails on chalkboard

364. Star girl unicorn

365. Magnificent Maleficient

366. Math homework

367. School science project

368. Haunted house

369. Ventriloquist with creepy dummy

370. An invisible person

371. The Shoveler

372. The Mask from the movie *The Mask*

373. Dragon queen

374. Werewolf Mailman

375. Hot rod Transformer

376. Can of worms

377. Kidnapped by aliens and replaced with a clone

378. Bad guy whose powers are derived from pocket watches

379. Dangerous Lumberjack

380. Bad wedding planner

381. Screenwriter who thinks she's trapped in a movie

382. A random assortment of junk you found in the garage

383. Pool boy

384. Popular Twitter post

385. Delicious burrito

386. Removed from Facebook group

387. Dog with three heads

388. E.T. and kid on a bicycle

389. Overly energetic yoga instructor

390. Single serving coffee pot

391. The balloon house from *Up*

392. Pharaoh king

393. Jessica and Roger Rabbit

394. League of Legends

395. Little Red Riding Hood but this time she eats the wolf

396. Ewoks with foam rocks to throw at people

397. Karate Kidder (tells a lot of bad jokes)

398. Oversized disco ball

399. Female Captain America

400. The number 400

401. Street rat Aladdin. Halfway through the night, you switch to Prince Ali.

402. The Ark of the Covenant

403. Mr. and Mrs. Potato Head

404. Ru-fi-oooooo!

405. Miami Vice detective

406. Bump in the night

407. Lion tamer that isn't very good at his job

408. Professional skateboarder

409. 50s diner milkshake dude

410. Nacho Libre sponsored by Taco Bell

411. Famous science fiction author Kilgore Trout

412. Black widow both the spider and the super hero

413. Mafia assassin

414. Evil tree

415. Paper bag princess

416. Over your data limit

417. Robot Cleopatra

418. Obscure character from a cult classic like *The Big Lebowsky*

419. Costume with Nintendo gun and SNES bazooka

420. Yes there was a bazooka

421. Free prize in cereal box

422. Barber who bakes people into pies

423. Spooky Woody and Creepy Buzz Lightyear

424. 80s workout clothing

425. Vegan hamburger

426. Jack Sparrow, but more bird than pirate

427. Turkey feathers

428. Grease monkey

429. Glinda the Bad Witch

430. Oktoberfest

431. Jafar

432. Star Trek alternate reality

433. The funny looking dudes from *Galaxy Quest*

434. Vampire aristocrat

435. Rainbow Power Ranger

436. Mad Hatter

437. Anime character with a sweet neon hairdo

438. Catwoman replaces Batman as the hero

439. Social Justice Warrior

440. Locked internet post

441. Power-tripping internet moderator

442. Ghosted on social media

443. Space Jam Bunny

444. Marry Me Poppins

445. Young Hagrid

446. Voodoo Doctor

447. First Person Shooter

448. Gaston vs the Beast

449. Harley Quinn, candy vendor and ex supervillain

450. Monday morning

451. The good, the bad, and the ugly

452. Called into work early

453. Dog ate my homework

454. Janitor Man, Janitor Man

455. Leaky can of gasoline

456. No cell phone reception

457. Cracked windshield

458. Football player who prefers another sport

459. Crazy cheerleader

460. Working late on a Friday

461. Queen of Spades

462. Poker face

463. Christmas elf that snaps and goes bananas

464. Thanks, Obama

465. Greek God of spit-roasted meat

466. Zaphod Beeblebrox

467. An android

468. The end of time

469. Journalist sick of writing clickbait so she snaps

470. Guy who brings acoustic guitar to every party

471. 80s news anchor

472. Daycare worker who eats the kids because she a monster

473. Biggest catfish ever

474. Mix tape for your gf

475. Country music star

476. Kangaroo boxer

477. Wooden robot

478. Duffman and Wife

479. Bears, beats, Battlestar Galactica

480. Louisiana hot sauce

481. Hotter than the mild sauce

482. Restaurant filled with noisy kids and maybe a biker gang

483. Bladerunner

484. Non-alcoholic beer

485. Vermont state trooper

486. Oscar winning movie

487. The Blair Witch Project

488. Dinosaur themed birthday party

489. Michael Jackson but you can only moonwalk

490. Bugs and cockroaches

491. Famous superhero Mintberry Crunch

492. Female rock band

493. Toaster falls into bathtub

494. Awesome soap opera

495. Kids cartoon show but more like *The Ring*

496. Lactose-intolerant volcano god

497. Dodgeball team

498. Cheerful undertaker

499. Kid on a milk carton

500. Canada goose

Made in the USA
Monee, IL
10 November 2019